Life's BIG Little Moments

SISTERS

Life's BIG Little Moments

SISTERS

SUSAN K. HOM

STERLING

New York / London
www.sterlingpublishing.com

For my sister, Jamie, with love

STERLING and the distinctive Sterling logo are registered trademarks of
Sterling Publishing Co., Inc.

Library of Congress Cataloging-in-Publication Data
Hom, Susan K.
  Life's big little moments : sisters / Susan K. Horn.
      p. cm.
  ISBN-13: 978-1-4027-4320-7
  ISBN-10: 1-4027-4320-3
  1. Sisters--Miscellanea. I. Title.

  HQ759.96.H66 2007
  306.875'4--dc22
                                        2007008213
10 9 8 7 6 5 4 3 2 1

Published by Sterling Publishing Co., Inc.
387 Park Avenue South, New York, NY 10016
© 2007 by Sterling Publishing Co., Inc.
Distributed in Canada by Sterling Publishing
c/o Canadian Manda Group, 165 Dufferin Street
Toronto, Ontario, Canada M6K 3H6
Distributed in the United Kingdom by GMC Distribution Services
Castle Place, 166 High Street, Lewes, East Sussex, England BN7 1XU
Distributed in Australia by Capricorn Link (Australia) Pty. Ltd.
P.O. Box 704, Windsor, NSW 2756, Australia

Cover and interior design by 3+Co. (www.threeandco.com)

Printed in China

Sterling ISBN-13: 978-1-4027-4320-7
         ISBN-10: 1-4027-4320-3

For information about custom editions, special sales, premium and
corporate purchases, please contact Sterling Special Sales
Department at 800-805-5489 or specialsales@sterlingpub.com.

Introduction

A sister isn't just a lifelong best friend, she is also family. She is a confidant, brutally honest shopping critic, and fellow comrade in family disagreements. You can share things with her that you can't share with even your mother or close friends. A sister offers both female empathy and a family member's unconditional love.

Your big sister will be there when you are dragging around a security blanket and when you have your first crush. Your little sister will help you celebrate joyful milestones like your graduation and wedding. Sisters will also be there for each other, with a box of tissues and lots of hugs, through tough times.

Your sister will understand what you're going through because she has weathered similar storms. In all of life's BIG little moments, it's clear that friends may come and go, but sisters are forever.

Little sisters show big sisters

the latest dance moves.

Big sisters teach little sisters

that they don't have to wait

for a boy to ask them to dance.

Big sisters stand behind little sisters

through thick and thin.

Little sisters inspire big sisters

to be good role models.

Sisters

balance each other.

Sisters show each other

how to enjoy every moment.

Big sisters encourage little sisters

to be themselves.

Little sisters remind big sisters

that talking to boys is easy.

Sisters motivate one another

to do their best.

Sisters are honest with each other

when one asks

"Do these jeans make me look fat?"

Sisters know each other intimately,

even if they live far apart.

Sisters

complement each other.

Big sisters tell little sisters

the latest jokes.

Little sisters show big sisters

how much fun it is

to share their space.

Little sisters encourage big sisters
to be more spontaneous.
Big sisters guide little sisters
during every step of life.

Sisters come together

during big and little moments.

Sisters encourage each other

to believe in a bright future.

Big sisters remind little sisters

who is in charge.

Little sisters require that big sisters

learn to be patient.

Big sisters show little sisters

how to make up silly games.

Little sisters remind big sisters

to make goofy faces

every now and then.

Sisters encourage each other

to share their thoughts.

Sisters rejoice

in each other's little victories.

Sisters start

each day with a hug.

Sisters teach each other

about togetherness.

Sisters

forgive each other.

Sisters love each other

no matter what.

Sisters show each other

how to be the life of the party.

Sisters remind each other

that it's fun to sing out loud.

Big sisters encourage little sisters

to love themselves.

Little sisters remind big sisters

to smile more often.

Sisters tell each other

not to worry.

Sisters remind each other

to laugh at their mistakes.

Big sisters encourage little sisters

to boogie down.

Little sisters remind big sisters

to dance barefoot once in a while.

Sisters inspire each other

to achieve their goals.

Sisters comfort each other

during their disappointments.

Little sisters remind big sisters

to be creative.

Big sisters help little sisters

discover who they are.

Big sisters teach little sisters

to be quiet when sneaking a cookie.

Little sisters warn big sisters

to not be greedy.

Sisters

compliment each other.

Sisters

look out for one another.

Sisters confide in each other

about their secret crushes.

Sisters reassure each other

that there will always

be room for girl time.

Big sisters

believe in their little sisters.

Little sisters

provide strong shoulders

to lean on, too.

Sisters laugh at each other's jokes,

even the stupid ones.

Sisters can

talk for hours.

Big sisters teach little sisters

to try new things.

Little sisters inspire big sisters

to be thoughtful.

Sisters

take care of each other.

Sisters

show each other

how to be courageous.

Big sisters

look out for little sisters.

Little sisters

teach big sisters to

cherish their time together.

Little sisters motivate big sisters

to take risks.

Big sisters show little sisters

how to face the unexpected.

Sisters encourage each other

to never give up.

Sisters inspire each other

to be more generous.

Little sisters remind big sisters

to enjoy splashing in the water.

Big sisters show little sisters

the way home.

Sisters give each other

spontaneous hugs and kisses.

Sisters

support one another.

Little sisters remind big sisters

how wonderful it is

to play in the sand.

Big sisters show little sisters

how to keep the sand

off their popsicles.

Little sisters tell big sisters

important news first.

Big sisters reassure little sisters

that their secrets are safe.

Sisters reminisce

about funny childhood memories.

Sisters remind one another

how good it feels to laugh.

Big sisters keep

little sisters safe.

Little sisters

trust in their big sisters.

Big sisters teach little sisters

that the icing is the yummiest part.

Little sisters help big sisters

eat all of the cake.

Big sisters reassure little sisters
that even when they fight,
they will still love each other.
Little sisters remind big sisters
that hugs are more powerful
than words.

Little sisters reassure big sisters

that they will always

have a movie buddy.

Big sisters coach little sisters

on how to play

their favorite sports.

Big sisters cheer up little sisters

on rainy days.

Little sisters show big sisters

that they're special just by

spending time with them.

Sisters remind each other

that their bond is strong.

Sisters encourage each other

to let their guard down.

Big sisters tell little sisters

that they are special.

Little sisters look to big sisters

to lead the way.

Big sisters tell little sisters

stories of enchanted lands
filled with fairies.

Little sisters encourage big sisters

to hold onto their wonder.

Photo Credits